LOVING YOU

LOVING YOU

Discovering the Meaning of "Together"

Written by Arthur Boze

Photography by Harv Gariety

♛ Hallmark Crown Editions

Set in Jeannette, a light, informal script
designed exclusively for Hallmark by Hermann Zapf.
Printed on Crown Royale Book paper.
Designed by Beth Hedstrom.

LOVING YOU

You happened...
and I found out that love is real....

Today is yesterday's tomorrow...

...and all that I had hoped for.

I love your loving me....
It's like being in a shower of flowers.

We keep saying, "I love you..."

...and I tell myself this can't last....

Yet, each day you still smile...

...and forever comes happily closer!

Being with you,

I feel like a cup of love bubbling over....

Your smile turns me upside down....
I walk on my hands among the clouds
shouting your name!

The sound of your voice is
my favorite music.
Listening to you I hear love's
symphony played just for me....

If I could fly I would soar into the clouds
and sculpture one in your image!
Then, all eyes could see your beauty.

Walking in the rain wasn't something I liked to do—
until you came along to hold my hand....

It's nice being loved by you.

It's been a long time since someone cared enough
to want to know when I would return
from wherever I went without them.

I feel lonesome when we're apart.
You were gone for four days once,
and it seemed like forty.

In my lonely daydreams
I was the only one aboard the ark
without a mate....

I worry when you're late,

afraid some accident has taken you from me.

I would knock on wood all day

if it would keep you safe.

Isn't it nice to come home to someone who loves you —
when the day of parting is unknown
and may never be!

If only time would drift away
and we could stay young for eternity
...keeping love's death
at bay....

Sometimes I close myself.
I go behind my private door
and contemplate life's funny ways.

I leave a peephole to see who's knocking...

but you're the only one who has a key.

I become fearful when you frown,

afraid I've done something wrong

to chase your smile away from me,

forever....

I would much rather see you happy—
I feel secure then.
There's a whole life to be lost in your frowns.

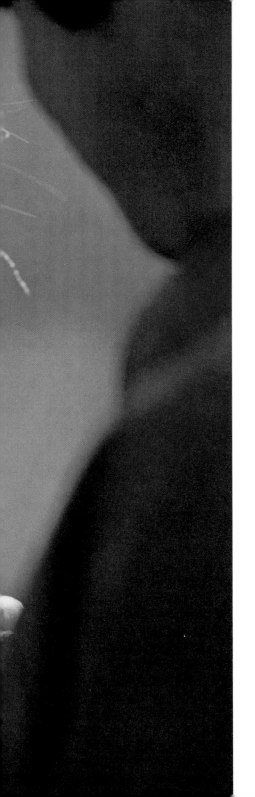

I love you...
you mean more to me than me.

You and I and love...

...soft, sweet trinity....

If I had my choice of Christmas presents,
  I would give myself you
      and years and years of your love....

Falling into sleep beside you
I close my eyes and feel your love surround me
like a warm spring day.

When we kiss,

our lips, touching,

whisper a thousand words of love....

In the park today we sat on cold stone benches
and ate the candy we had just bought —

chocolate creams and caramels with nuts...

...but you tasted sweeter....

Between us there is gentleness.

Our silences lie softly....

I didn't think I would ever find
anyone who was perfect for me.
You're a surprise to my life...
...a sun to light up my world.

You ask me why I love you
and I don't really know what to say.
Except that you're the sum of a lot of things
I need to make me happy.

I've fallen completely in love with you...

even my shadow follows yours!